This book is dedicated to my sister, Nancy, who has been my lifelong friend and inspiration.

You can choose your friends.

Family is a gift to be treasured loved and enjoyed.

All rights reserved. You may tat as many of the items from these patterns as you wish and may sell your tatted items or give them away. You may NOT copy, modify, or distribute these patterns in any way without prior written permission of the author.

Copyright © 2009 Ruth Perry Rozella Linden Tatting
First Printing 2009
Linden Publishing
Lebanon, Ohio
Revised Edition
Copyright © 2014 Ruth Perry - Rozella Linden Tatting
ISBN-13: 978-1492796992
ISBN-10: 1492796999

Celtic Tatted Leaves and Flowers

Introduction

As a young child, I was always fascinated by anything in nature. From flowers to worms, and horses to bugs: if it was nature I loved it. I wanted to bring worms in the house to give them a bath in the tub because my mother told me they were dirty. She did not appreciate my reasoning!

However, I was allowed to bring in flowers and leaves. My favorite flowers were the beautiful yellow Dandy Lions that flourished throughout our yard and the maple leaves from the trees in the front yard. I just loved the colors and shapes!

Delicate willow leaves, beautiful buckeye leaves, huge catalpa leaves, oaks, maples, elm, and tulip, iris, gladiola, daffodil and rose leaves all were readily available on our street in Warren Ohio. Of course, I had a leaf collection. Each of them was carefully pressed between two pieces of wax paper and glued into a scrapbook.

They lasted for a while, but eventually crumbled into dust. These tatted leaves should last a lifetime. Hopefully they will bring a smile to the face of many people who share my love for the shapes and colors of nature and an appreciation of the Celtic designs and knot work.

Many leaf shapes may also be used as flower petal shapes and wing shapes for insects, angels, and fairies. Let your imagination guide you in adding these leaves to your tatted flowers and other creations. For more information about botany of leaves and leaf shapes, go to

http://botany.com/leaf.html

Terms & Notation

DS	Tatting stitch or double stitch
BDS	Balanced double stitch - see appendix for details of BDS
RDS	Reverse Double Stitch or direct tatting or wrapped stitches or encapsulation like the second half of a split ring.
-	Picot
+ or Join	join to a previously tatted picot
Ring (2 – 2)	Tat a ring with 2ds, a picot, then 2ds, and then close the ring
turn	Reverse work or flip it over top to bottom
CTM	Continuous Thread Method – do not cut the thread between the ball and shuttle
Chain ##	Tat a chain of ## ds [## indicates the number of ds to tat]
BOLD PRINT	Tatting instructions are in bold print; comments are not
{ }	Comments within instructions for a ring or chain
THC	Tie the thread ends. Hide the ends. Cut them off.
Overhand knot	A simple knot like used to tie your shoes
Double Overhand Knot	The same as the overhand knot except the thread goes through the middle two times before tightening the knot.

Table of Contents

Elm or Rose Leaf	2
Maple Leaf	4
Iris Leaf	8
Leaves of Loops	9
Poinsettia	10
Daffodil	15
Iris	21
Poppy	27
Rosebud	35
Rosebud Heart	39
Stargazer Lily	43
Day Lily	51
Star Flower	53
Dragonfly	54
Balanced Double Stitch	57

Helpful Hints

Tightly tatted chains that have DS pushed close together will have a curve in them that will make these Celtic tatted pieces look great and hold their shape. If your tatting is loose and floppy, work on improving your tension.

When doing the weaving, never twist or turn the chains like turning a book page. If the tatting does not lie flat check the weaving before moving on.

Examine your work for a spot where you missed crossing over correctly or twisted the chains. Fix the problem before moving on.

Diagrams

Some of the diagrams in this book are from scans or photos of the actual tatting with numbers placed over the tatting to indicate the number of stitches in a particular section of tatting. Some of the diagrams are drawings by Sparrow Kelley.

Below is the diagram for the Elm Leaf. There are numbers on the left side, but not on the right side. The stitch counts for the right side are the same because it is symmetrical.

The small ring of the outline row has the number 4 one time. This ring is actually Ring (4 + 4 + 4) but, since all the stitch counts are the same, the number is only shown one time.

Elm or Rose Leaf Celtic Twist

If you consider the outline of a leaf as the shape and the inside of the leaf a filler pattern, there are endless possibilities for tatting patterns by simply filling in the outline of the leaf with tatting.

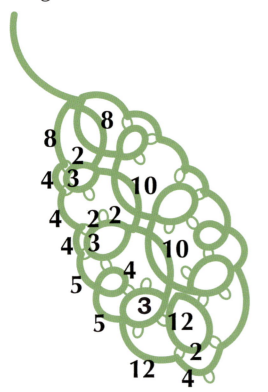

Celtic weaving and Celtic knots make beautiful and interesting fillers.

We will begin with a simple Celtic twist interlace pattern. Many of the leaves and petals are woven in this manner.

Instructions for weaving are pretty much the same, although the tatting instructions may differ to achieve different shapes and color combinations by tatting with variegated threads or using a different color for the ball thread and shuttle thread.

Here is a basic leaf shape, similar to a rose leaf or elm leaf. Begin a tatted chain with a picot at the beginning of the chain by tying a knot between the shuttle & ball, and then tat the first DS a picot's distance from the knot.

Tatting Instructions

Chain – 8 turn

Ring (2 – 3 – 3 – 2) turn

Chain 10 turn

Ring (2 – 2 – 3 – 3 – 2 – 2) turn

Chain 10 turn

Ring (2 – 2 – 3 – 3 – 2 – 2) turn

Chain 12 – 2 – 12 turn

Ring (2 – 2 – 3 – 3 – 2 – 2) turn

Chain 10 turn

Ring (2 – 2 – 3 – 3 – 2 – 2) turn

Chain 10 turn

Ring (2 – 3 – 3 – 2) turn

Chain 8

Weave the Celtic twist as shown in the instructions for the Maple Leaf on the following pages, and then join to the picot at the beginning of the first chain.

Outline Row

Chain 10 + 3 + 4 + 5 + 5 + turn

Ring (4 + 4 + 4) turn

Chain 5 + 4 + 12 + 4 – 4 + 12 + 4 + 5

The picot at the 4 – 4 is the point of the leaf. Continue tatting the other side of the leaf outline as a mirror image to complete the leaf.

Celtic Maple Leaf

This leaf was designed for the Fringe Element Tat Days event in Ontario, Canada 2008.

Instructions

All the rings in this pattern are the same as this first one:

Ring (2 – 1 – 1 – 1 – 1 – 2) turn

Chain 8 – 12 turn

Ring, turn

Chain 12 turn

Ring, turn

Chain 12 – 2 – 12 turn

Ring, turn

Chain 12 turn

Ring, turn

Chain 12

* * * * * * **STOP** * * * * * *

You may use one color on the shuttle and a different ball color as in the photo above, in which case, tat the first ring, then tat the first 8 DS over the ends and shuttle thread with the second color, then leave the ends out and continue tatting as shown below.

At this point, we will need to weave the tatted rings and chains into a Celtic design for the structure of the leaf.

Bend the tatting at the two picots and then cross the right side chain over the left, as shown here. Next, cross the chain that is now on the right side over the one on the left again. Continue doing this until the rings and chains are all interwoven and look like the photo below.

Turn it over and notice that the weave looks the same on both sides with the chains crossing over and under.

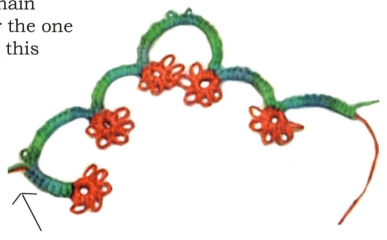

These thread ends are about 18" long

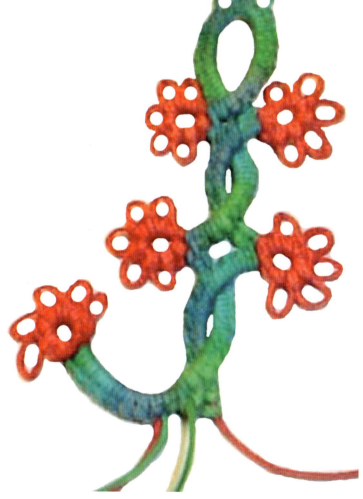

Now, join to the first picot and then continue tatting the next section of the Celtic weave for the center section of the leaf.

5

Chain 2 – 12 turn

Ring, turn

Chain 12 turn

Ring, turn

Chain 12 turn

Ring, turn

Chain 12 – 2 – 12 turn

Ring, turn

Chain 12 turn

Ring, turn

Chain 12 turn

Ring, turn

Chain 12

**** STOP ****

Weave the tatting for each rib of the leaf so that it looks like the photos. After weaving, join to the previous picot on the chain and then continue.

Ring (2 – 1 – 1 – 1 – 1 – 2) turn

Chain 8 – 12 turn

Ring, turn

Chain 12 turn

Ring, turn

Chain 12 – 2 – 12 turn

Ring, turn

Chain 12 turn

Ring, turn

Chain 12

Weave the piece as before, then join to the previous picot.

We now have completed the three main ribs of the leaf, and the first ring and chain make four of the five lines needed for the structure of the leaf.

Now, leave a thread space about the length of 8 DS, and tat the final ring. Tat over the ends 8 RDS.

Tie the shuttle thread end to the thread end left at the beginning, and the ball thread to the end left at the beginning.

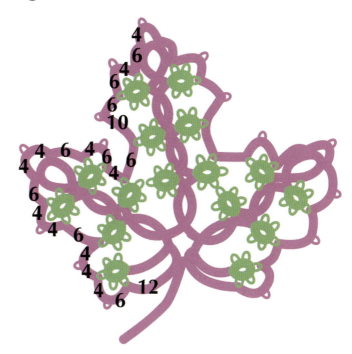

You may cut the shuttle and ball threads to the length of the thread ends left at the beginning. These ends may be used to make twisted cord for a bookmark when the leaf is finished.

Now tat around the outside of the leaf with the chain thread color on a shuttle CTM. Do not cut from the ball.

Outline Round

Chain 12 + 6 – 4 + 4 – 4 + 6 + 4 – 4 + 6 + 4 – 4 + 6 + 4 – 6 + 4+ 6 + 10 – 6 + 6 – 4 + 6 + 4 –

No two leaves are exactly the same in nature, so feel free to experiment with the outline of this leaf and make the second side slightly different than the first side of the outline. There is one difference between the right and left side in the drawing above. You may do it either the same or different.

When the outline is completed, tie the ends together and then finger tat over the rest of the thread ends with two of the ends. Tie all the ends in a double overhand knot, then make twisted cord with all the ends long enough for a bookmark. Tie another double overhand knot and trim the ends for a tassel about two inches long.

Daffodil Leaf or Iris Leaf

Tatting a long slender leaf presents an interesting challenge. The method we used in the previous two leaves will work to tat the leaf, but if the leaf is to stand up it must have some way to strengthen or stiffen it. One way would be to use a mixture of half white glue and half water. Soak the leaves in the solution, then block and allow drying completely.

My grandmother used sugar water or clothing starch to stiffen her doilies. I never starch my husband's shirts. That's why the shirt laundry service was invented. So, I don't keep a block of starch around the house. Sugar may attract ants or rodents. UGH !!!

Another way to hold these leaves upright would be to add wire to the tatting, as in this long straight leaf. I tatted the rings and chains with 12 rings on each side, and then did the Celtic weaving as before. I think there are about 12 DS in each of the chains in this sample.

To tat the outline of the leaf with wire inside requires shuttle and ball CTM and a strand of wire the desired gauge which is a little longer than twice the desired length of the finished leaf and stem.

The ball thread and wire are the core of the outline, and all the stitches are wrapped onto the core from the shuttle, like the second half of a split ring. I call these reverse double stitches or RDS. The second half is tatted first, but no flip. Then tat the first half with no flip.

To join to the rings of the inside of the leaf, you will pull the "ball" core thread up through the picot of the ring, then continue with the RDS to the next join, wrapping the stitches over the ball thread and the wire. If you look carefully at the photo above you can see the wire at the bottom of this leaf. This method may be used to add wire to the outline of any tatting without having to put wire on a tatting shuttle.

Detailed instructions for this leaf are on page 24 & 25.

To "fill" the inside of the leaf, tat many picots on the rings as in the sample on the right. These picots may be left intact or cut and then frayed to give a fuzzy or more solid look to the leaf.

Notice how this sample has a natural curve or skew to it. Simply grasp the outline at the top on one side and at the bottom on the other and pull gently.

Leaves of Loops

This arrowhead or heart-shaped leaf is very easy to tat. The inside of the leaf is just tatted chains that loop over and over in a Celtic loop pattern.

Morning Glory leaves are heart shaped. These leaves are tatted chains. Begin with a small amount of green thread on a shuttle, CTM. Do not cut the thread from the ball.

Put a paper clip on the thread between the ball and shuttle, or begin with a picot by making an overhand knot in the thread between the ball and shuttle, then make the first DS a picot's distance from the knot.

Chain – 15 – 20 – 20 – 20 – 15 +

This final join is to the picot at the beginning of the chain. The chains curve around in a Celtic weave as shown in the photo detail below. This is best tatted with fairly tight tension. Continue tatting the outline of the leaf.

Chain 20 + 10 + 10 – 10 + 10 + 20

The final join is to the beginning picot again. Tat two or more leaves and set them aside after tatting the vines about the same length as the leaf length. Add tatted spirals and tat over the ends. The Balanced Double Stitch [BDS] will allow the chains to bend in either direction. See the detailed instructions at the end of this book.

The Morning Glory flower pattern is on http://tatting.wordpress.com

Celtic Tatted Christmas Poinsettia

This is an advanced tatting project that requires weaving tatted Celtic knots.

The center flower is tatted split rings with "floating" rings and chains. The two rows of Celtic knot bracts are tatted in one round alternating a large and then a small one.

The yellow center of the Poinsettia is the flower. Center - Yellow Split Rings with "floating rings and chains" 2 shuttles [See diagram]

Ring #1 SR (2 – 2 / [The rest of this ring is the second half of the split ring]

*****
Leave about 1/8" and then tat a small ring with the second shuttle thread.

Ring (1 – 1 – 1 – 1 – 1 – 1) Five small picots with 1 DS between them.

Chain 3 RDS This chain is tatted over the 1/8th" of thread.

Tat on the center ring: (2 – 2) This is direct tatting or RDS.

Repeat from ***** until there are 5 floating rings and chains around the center split ring with a picot between 2 DS between each of them.) Close the ring and then tat one more chain and ring with the ends; then tie, cut and hide ends.

Celtic knots form the bracts of this bright Christmas Poinsettia. These are the red "petals" of the flower. They are not actually petals, but leaves or bracts that are red instead of green.

We are ready to tat the sixth chain and ring with the ends:

Chain 3 turn

Small ring (1 – 1 – 1 – 1 – 1 – 1) Close the ring.

THC Tie, Hide, and then cut the thread ends off close to the work.

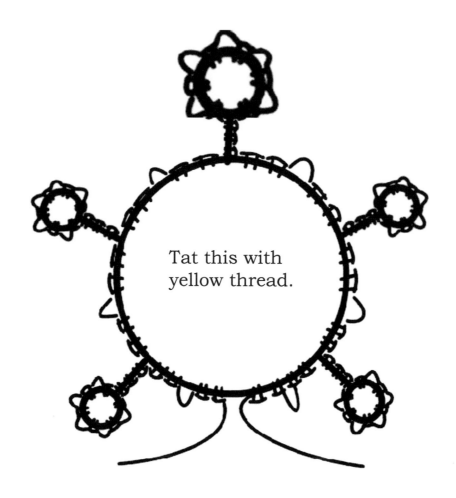

This drawing shows the first Center ring with five floating rings and encapsulated chains.

Second Center Ring with floating rings and chains (This ring will be used later when assembling the flower. It does not have the picots to attach the bracts.)

Split Ring (2 / *
{ floating ring and encapsulating chain as in previous ring} 2 *)

Repeat between * until there are five floating rings and chains with 2 DS between them.

Close the ring and tat a sixth floating ring and chain as in the first center ring. This ring is like the first, but smaller and without the 6 picots around. Set the second center ring aside for now.

Overlap (alligator) Join: Used at the base of each bract to continue tatting around the outside.

Bracts: Two Celtic Tatting shuttles wound continuous with red thread or finger tatting. Begin by joining the red thread to any one of the picots of the yellow center.

Large Petal (Bract)

Chain 25 – 25 – 5 – 5 – 25 – 25

Weave the Celtic Knot as shown below.

Tighten the knot so that it is in the center of the petal, and there is a point at each end.

Continue tatting: Join back into the same yellow picot as you began by placing the knotting thread under the beginning of the chain for this petal, and then using a crochet hook or the hook on a tatting shuttle to pull a small loop of the thread up through the picot. Insert the shuttle through the loop and then tighten the threads.

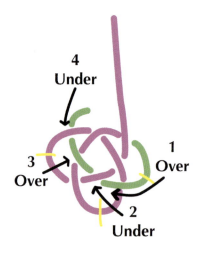

First half of DS made. Tat the second half of the DS as you normally would, and then continue tatting around the outside of the petal. Join made - see above.

The tatting continues in the same direction.

Chain 14 + 10 + 5 + 5 + 10 + 14

Join back in the same yellow picot as before.

(The number of DS can be adjusted for eye appeal if your tatting is loose.)

12

Small Petal (bract)

Chain 3 – 14 – 14 – 14

Weave the trefoil Celtic Knot. Join in the first picot of this petal as above. This trefoil knot is just an overhand knot tied in the tatted chain.

Chain 10 + 8 – 8 + 10

Tatted Sample

Join back in the same picot again and then continue tatting.

Chain 3

Join in the next picot of the yellow center and then tat another large petal. Continue tatting petals alternating large petals and small petals.

Cut tie and hide threads.

There will be six large petals and six small petals. Arrange the small petals on top of the large petals, so it looks like there are two rows of petals.

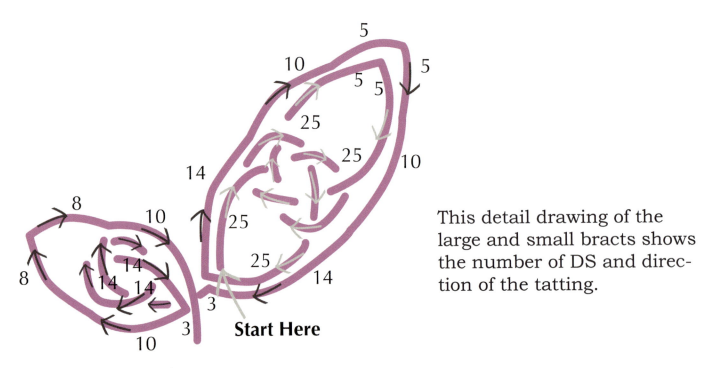

This detail drawing of the large and small bracts shows the number of DS and direction of the tatting.

Examine a live Poinsettia to observe the arrangement of the red and green leaf-shaped bracts. They are often many different sizes. This can be done by varying the stitch count in some of the additional leaves if desired.

An entire Poinsettia plant could be tatted with the flowers and leaves on floral wire stems wrapped with floral tape to hide the thread ends.

Assembling the Poinsettia

Use green thread on two shuttles CTM.
Tat a small ring to start.

Ring (5 – 5)

Insert the ends of this green ring through the hole in the center of the smaller yellow ring. Next, insert all the thread ends through the center of the yellow ring with the petals attached.

Tat a green ring with a row of just the large petals. Increase the number of DS for the petals as desired to make these green leaves larger, and make either three or six leaves in this row. The only real difference between the red "petals" and green "leaves" of the poinsettia is the color.

Online information about the legend of the Poinsettia is available here:
http://www.appleseeds.org/poinsettia-legend.htm

Celtic Knot Tatted Daffodil

This beautiful spring flower is tatted in three pieces which are then joined together and may be attached to a floral wire stem.

The six flower petals are two groups of three petals. The upright part of the flower is tatted as three Celtic knot sections woven together at the sides as the piece is tatted.

Then a final row is tatted around the top which secures the three Celtic Knot sections together.

Use size 20 or larger thread in yellow, but some daffodils have a little white or orange which may be used for the final row around the top. Floral wire stem and floral tape will finish off the flower to use in an arrangement.

The daffodil is an advanced Celtic knot tatting project that will require time and patience as well as tatting expertise to complete.

Instructions

Petals - Shuttle and Ball CTM

Chain 2 – 2 – 8 turn

Ring (1 – 1 – 1 – 1 – 1 – 1) turn

Chain 10 turn

Ring (1 – 1 – 1 – 1 – 1 – 1) turn

Chain 10 turn

Ring (1 – 1 – 1 – 1 – 1 – 1) turn

Chain 6 – 2 – 6 turn [Point of petal]

Ring (1 – 1 – 1 – 1 – 1 – 1) turn

Chain 10 turn

Ring (1 – 1 – 1 – 1 – 1 – 1) turn

Chain 10 turn

Ring (1 – 1 – 1 – 1 – 1 – 1) turn

Chain 8

Ring (1 – 1 – 1 – 1 – 1 – 1) turn

Chain 10 turn

Ring (1 – 1 – 1 – 1 – 1 – 1) turn

Chain 6 – 2 – 6 turn [Point of petal]

Ring (1 – 1 – 1 – 1 – 1 – 1) turn

Chain 10 turn

Ring (1 – 1 – 1 – 1 – 1 – 1) turn

Chain 10 turn

Ring (1 – 1 – 1 – 1 – 1 – 1) turn

Chain 8

> Weave this petal similar to the elm, maple and iris leaf.
>
> Join to the second picot at the beginning of the petal in an "alligator" type join. See the alligator join diagram on page 12.

Middle Row

Chain 8 + 2 – 2 – 2 – 2 – 2 + 2 – 2 – 2 – 2 – 2 – 2 + 2 – 2 – 2 – 2 +

Chain 2 – 2 – 2 – 2 – 2 – 2 + [Point of petal]

Chain 2 – 2 – 2 – 2 + 2 – 2 – 2 – 2 – 2 – 2 + 2 – 2 – 2 – 2 – 2 – 2 + 8

Join to the first picot at the beginning of the petal in an "alligator" type join.

Outside Row

Chain 10 + 5 + 5 turn

Ring (3 + 2 + 3) turn

Chain 5 + 5 + 5 + 5 + 5 + –

[Point of petal] leave a small picot at the join here. Continue tatting around the outside of the petal.

Chain 5 + 5 + 5 + 5 + 5

Ring (3 + 2 + 3) turn

Chain 5 + 5 + 10

Tie the shuttle and ball thread at the join to the first picot of this petal, then

Chain 3 DS

Repeat these instructions two more times for a group of three petals.

When three petals have been tatted, tie, hide, and cut the threads close to the work.

Repeat the instructions for a second group of three petals. Place one group of three petals over the other with the petals making a six-point star shape. Baste them in place with a contrasting thread that will be easy to remove later.

Daffodil Center

Begin a tatted chain on a paper clip or tie an overhand knot in the thread between the shuttle and ball. The first double stitch is tatted about the distance of a picot from the knot. This will create a small picot at the beginning of the chain which will be used for joining later.

Chain – 20 – 20 – 20 – 20 – 20 – 20

(This is 1 picot at the beginning, then 5 picots sep by 20 DS)

Weave the chains into the Celtic knot as shown. The first section is easy: just weave the beginning of the chain through. Start where indicated and follow the arrows, ending back where you began at the other end of the chain.

Tie the ends at the beginning to hold everything in place. The "over, under, over, under" pattern of Celtic knots makes it easy to tell that everything is correct when the knot is completed.

^ Start Here

18

Petal Outline

Tat a chain around the outside of the Celtic Knot for the outline of the petal.

Chain 10 + 10
Join to the first picot on one side of the Celtic Knot.

Ring (6 + 3 – 3)
Join to the next picot on the Celtic Knot

Chain 2 – 2 – 2 – 2 – 2 – 2

Ring (3 + 3 + 3 – 3)
Join to the picot of the previous ring and to the picot of the center loop of the Celtic knot.

Chain 2 – 2 – 2 – 2 – 2 – 2

Ring (3 + 3 + 6)
Join to the picot of the previous ring and the picot at the point of the next loop of the Celtic knot.

Chain 10 + 10
Join to the picot on the end of the next loop of the Celtic knot.

Finally join back to the picot at the beginning of this row.

One section completed.

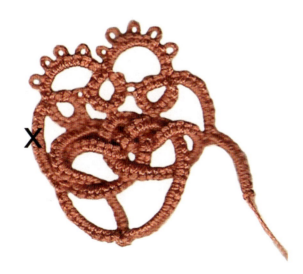

Chain 2 DS

Now repeat the previous instructions for the second section, but also weave the chain of the outside row through the corresponding chain of the first section. The sample here shows how it should look before the final join.

The X marks where the next section will weave through this one. The chain following the third ring of the next section will go over, then under through the space by the X.

This is difficult to photograph because of the 3-D shape formed when the final join is made. It is shown here flattened out, but that makes the chains look crumpled up. The actual piece will begin to have a bowl shape.

Repeat again for the third section which weaves through both the second section on one side, and the first section on the other. This creates a "bell" shape made with three tatted Celtic Knots.

Final top row

Shuttle and ball CTM with yellow, white, orange, or variegated thread.

Ring (4 + 4 + 4) turn
This ring joins to one picot of each of two Celtic knot sections.

Chain 2 – 2 – 2 – 2 – 2 – 2 +
Join to the middle picot of upper chain of the Celtic knot section.

Chain 2 – 2 – 2 – 2 – 2 – 2 +
Join to the middle picot of upper chain of the next Celtic knot section.

Repeat around the top of the center. Tie the ends at the beginning of this row. Hide the ends and cut close to the work. The burnt orange sample on page 20 shows more contrast and therefore is easier to see. The final row holds the three separate sections of the center together at the top.

When the flower is finished, remove the basting around the petals that you did earlier in a contrasting color. If you wish, you may sew them together with matching thread that does not need to be removed.

Assemble the flower by inserting the thread ends of the center through the middle of the two groups of three petals. Secure the petals in place as shown for the Lily pattern on page 48.

Celtic Knot Iris

Iris come in many different varieties that grace the garden with blooms throughout most of the summer months.

The bearded iris is one of the most spectacular, because of the feathery "beard" near the base of the downward-turned petals.

To learn more about iris visit
http://worldiris.com

There is often prominent veining in the petals of this flower, which lends itself to the graceful shapes of Celtic Knots. This is art not photography.

The finished piece will be obviously an iris, but in a side-by-side comparison, the live flower and our tatted one will not be identical.

In nature, no two objects are exactly alike, not even two blossoms on the exact same plant. I expect that each person who tats this flower to make it his or her own, different size picots, different thread size, perhaps different stitch counts to allow for the best fit with the thread used.

It's OK to be different. In fact, it's a very good thing.

Supplies needed:

Tatting shuttle or needle or finger tatting. Hook to do joins. Scissors to cut thread. Thread in colors of your choice. (Suggestion - size 10 in purple, lavender, and yellow) Also: cloth-covered flower stem wire, floral tape, tissue paper, and paddle wire to stiffen the outline of the leaves (optional)

The most important requirement is patience, and more patience. Long tatted chains have the final shape tatted in because of the shaping and tension of the tatting. Tight tatting works best. Needle tatting tends to be looser, and may require stiffening.

INSTRUCTIONS:

Wind two shuttles CTM (continuous thread method) with the color to be used for the center of the lower petals. Begin a tatted chain on a paper clip, or tie an overhand knot in the thread between the shuttles. The first double stitch is tatted about the distance of a picot from the knot. This will create a small picot at the beginning of the chain which will be used for joining later.

Shuttle one Chain (20 – 20 – 20 – 20 – 20 – 20)

(This is 5 picots sep by 20 DS)

Weave the chains into the Celtic Knot. Position a picot at the middle of every loop. Start where indicated and follow the arrows, ending back where you began at the other end of the chain. Tie the ends in a square knot to hold everything in place.

^ Start Here

BEARD

Next, add a piece of thread about a yard long for the BEARD, and tat a chain with 15 picots each separated by one DS. Repeat this with the other shuttle, making sure that the beard color is the "ball" thread for both sides of the beard.

PETAL OUTLINE

Tat a chain around the outside of the beard and Celtic Knot for the outline of the petal.

Chain (15 + 10 + 10)
Join to a picot on the beard closest to the Celtic Knot, and then to the first picot on one side of the Celtic Knot.

Ring (6 + 3 – 3)
Join to the next picot on the Celtic Knot

Chain (10)

Ring (3 + 3 + 3 – 3)
Join to the picot of the previous ring, and to the picot of the center loop of the Celtic Knot.

Chain (10)

Ring (3 + 3 + 6)
Join to the picot of the previous ring and the picot at the point of the next loop of the Celtic Knot.

Chain (10 + 10 + 15)
Join to the picot on the end of the next loop of the Celtic Knot, to a picot of the beard, and then tie the thread ends in square knots matching like colors.

Next tat a chain with 25 picots separated by 1 DS and join the end back into the base of the petal. This is the "cap" that goes over the beard.

Tat two more petals that look the same as this first one, and then three without the beard for the center. Gather the ends of the center petals which will stand upright, and insert them between the three bottom petals.

Add a flower stem, and wrap with floral tape. A bit of tissue paper at the bottom of the flower looks like the thin covering at the base of live iris.

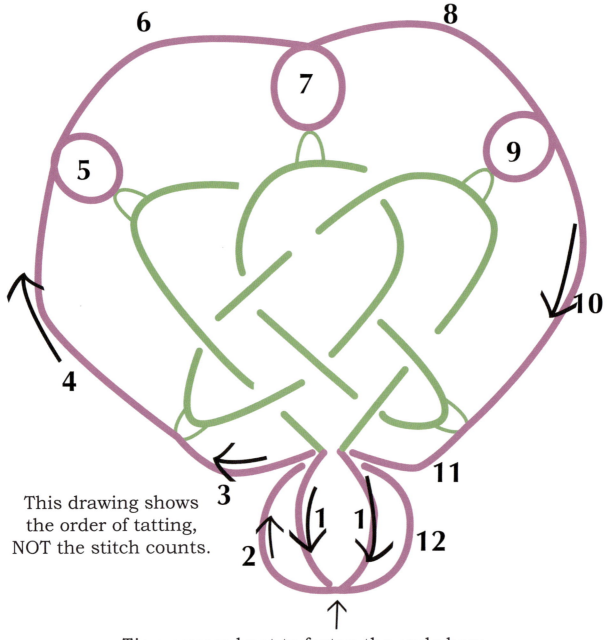

This drawing shows the order of tatting, NOT the stitch counts.

Tie a square knot to fasten the ends here.

24

The previous drawing is not to the exact scale, but shows where the tatting around the knot goes. This piece will "cup" or draw up around the outside when the last two joins are done. It seems like the row around the outside is too short, but this is what gives the shape of the petals.

Adding lots of picots around the outline will give a ruffled appearance which some iris exhibit. Some are very plain around the edge. The upper three petals do not have the beard. Skip steps one, two, and twelve for these three petals. The lower three "petals" have the beard, and after tatting around the entire petal as shown here, tat the "cap" over the petals that starts and ends at the same spot. Tie the ends together in a square knot again after tatting the cap.

Iris leaf

An iris leaf is long and slender. Tat any edging in green thread, and then tat around the outside of this with the same green, but encapsulate (tat over wire) a piece of wire so that the leaf will stand upright.

Chain (3 – 1 – 1 – 6) turn

Ring (3 – 3) turn

Chain (8) turn

Ring (3 – 3) turn

Chain (8) turn

Ring (3 – 3) turn

Repeat rings and chains to desired length

Chain (6 – 2 – 6) turn

Ring (3 – 3) turn

Continue back down the other side matching the number of rings and chains. Bend in the center as shown here, weave one side over the other, join, and tat around the outside over wire.

Tat 7 picots separated by 1 DS at the point between the 2P.

The Celtic Twist pattern shown here makes a beautiful Iris leaf. Tat over wire and around the outside of this and join to each ring.

This is similar to the leaf on page 8 and the Leaves and Petals of the Lily patterns added in this revised edition.

Twist Weave & Alligator Join

Celtic Poppy Flower

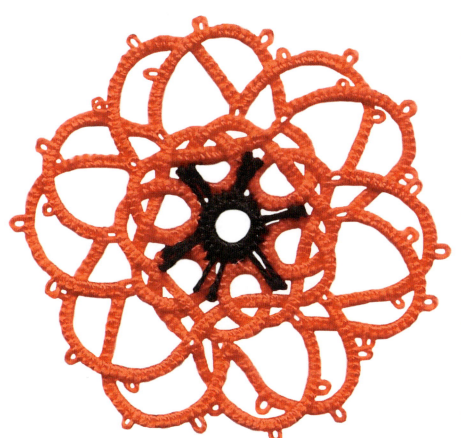

Poppy flowers have a dark center with bright orange, red, yellow, pink or purple petals.

This tatted version is a somewhat difficult piece to do. It is for those who wish to take on a challenge!

There are basically three parts to tatting the poppy: the dark center, the Celtic knot work around the center, and the Celtic interlace petals around the outside.

The sample shown here is tatted in DMC Perle Cotton size 8 thread. It is about 2" in diameter finished size.

It took me about two hours to tat this flower, and it's kind of fiddley because weaving the chains into the Celtic knot requires patience. Two Celtic type shuttles are highly recommended, but it can be done with finger tatting.

Poppy Flower 3-D makes a nice size Fashion Doll Hat

Instructions

Center

Start with about a yard of black or a dark color of thread on any tatting shuttle. The center is done as a double core reversed ring, meaning that the thread goes through the center twice, and all the stitches are direct tatted like the second half of a split ring.

Grab the thread about 5 inches from the end, and wrap it around your hand two times then back through the pinch. Tat second half first with no flip, then the first half with no flip. lp is a long picot about 3/4 inch.

Ring (2 – 2 lp 2 – 2 lp 2 – 2 lp 2 – 2 lp 2 – 2 lp 2 – 2)

There are 6 regular picots and 5 long picots. The sixth long picot will be the thread ends after the ring is closed.

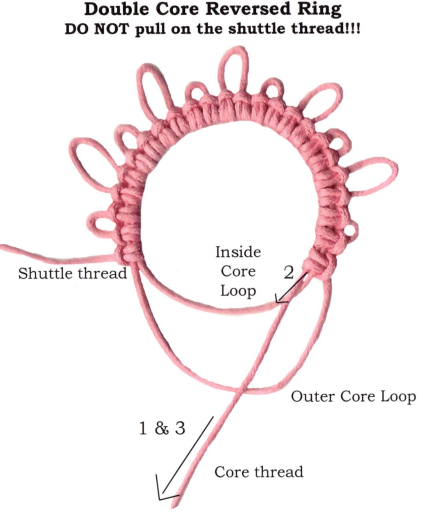

**Double Core Reversed Ring
DO NOT pull on the shuttle thread!!!**

The core thread end is the end left before wrapping the thread around your hand.

1. Pull the core thread end about an inch or two to identify the inside core loop.

2. The inside core loop that is shorter now is the one to pull to close the outer core loop. Pull on it gently until the outer core loop is closed.

3. Pull the core thread end to close the inside core loop. This will close the ring completely. Cut both of the thread ends to about the length of the long picots. There are no thread ends to hide for the center.

28

Center ring option two

This is a normal ring, but there are thread ends to hide.

Ring (2 – 4 – 4 – 4 – 4 – 4 – 2)

Close the ring and hide the ends, then cut the ends off close to the work.

Celtic interweave around the center

This round is tatted in two steps. The first time around, start with thread on any shuttle with ball thread CTM. Start with a picot by tying an overhand knot in the thread between the ball and shuttle, and then tat the first DS a picot's distance from the knot.

Chain – 20 – 12 – 4 + 4 – 12 – 20 – 12 – 4 + 4 – 12 – 20 -- 12 – 4 + 4 – 12

Tie the end to the beginning picot, and then wrap the shuttle and ball thread onto a thread holder with about three yards. of ball thread available cut from the ball of thread. This thread will be used for the petals around the outside.

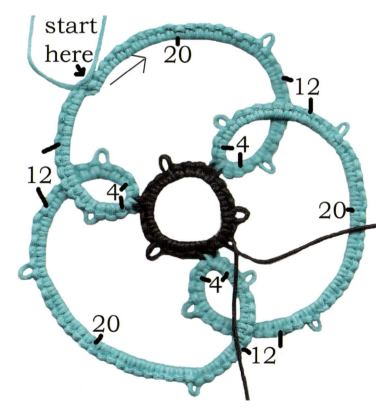

This photo shows the second option for the center ring, but I haven't hidden the thread ends yet.

The joins are to every other picot of the center ring. The chain stitches are all pushed together tightly so that the chain holds the shape as shown.

Notice how every one of the loops of chain cross over under the same way. It is necessary that all of the chains, loops, and weaving be exactly as shown.

The second time around is more tricky because of the weaving through the previous chain loops. Begin with the thread on two Celtic style tatting shuttles that are CTM and full of thread so that there is enough thread to tat this round and the petals.

Chain - 12 + 4 + 4 + 12 – 20 – 12 + 4 + 4 + 12 – 20 – 12 + 4 + 4 + 12 – 20

Notice that this chain begins with a picot and then 12 stitches instead of the 20 we did the first time around! The joins are to the picots of the previous chain, center ring, previous chain.

Weave the chains as you go along being careful that each weave is exactly as shown. When you have finished this round, it will have the look of a true Celtic knot with no place where the chains cross over - over, or under - under. All the weaving is over under over under.

The sample is shown here in three colors for clarity.

Perhaps the first practice piece should be tatted with large thread (size 10) in three colors so that you understand how to do the weaving.

Using large thread will also make it easier for you to see what you are doing.

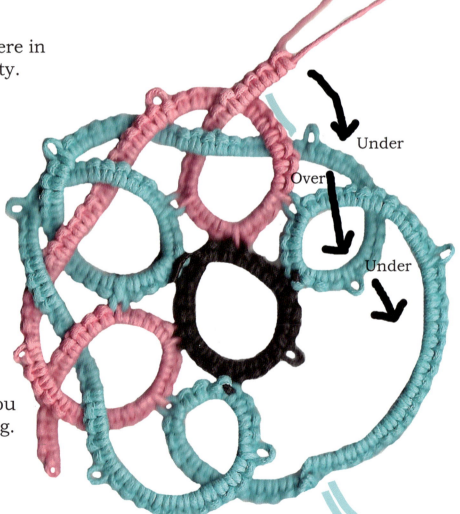

30

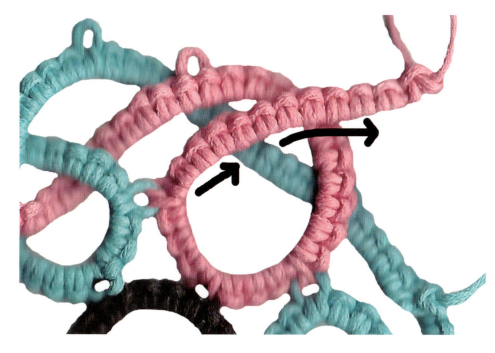

Weave the pink chain under the blue and then back over the pink as shown by the arrows.

The detail photo above shows how it looks when we are ready to weave the pink chain that was just tatted under the blue chain from the previous pass of this round.

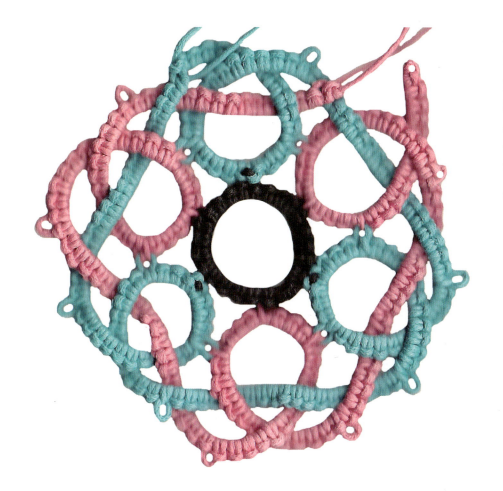

All of the weaving is completed in this photo. There are 5 more stitches to tat, and then join the end to the picot at the beginning of this pass around the center.

Check that all the weaving is perfect before tying the end of this chain to the beginning picot.

Petals

This round is also tatted in two passes. The first with the two Celtic shuttles used in the previous step.

Chain 8 – 8 – 8 – 8 +

Join to the picot of the previous round that is the second one past where the chain begins.

Repeat this around skipping every other picot.

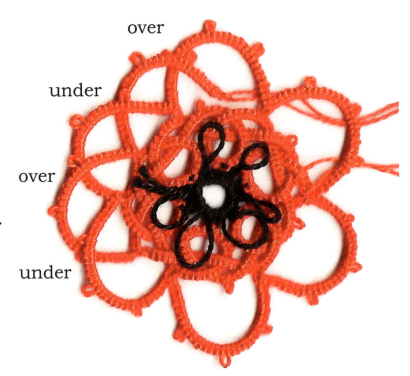

The photo on the right shows the final round of petals started. After tatting the chain section, but before the join to the previous round, put the Celtic shuttles through the petal - front to back. Then do the join and continue tatting the next petal.

Final Round of Petals

This time around use the threads from the first pass of the previous round on two Celtic type shuttles. Join to the skipped picots of the previous round.

Chain 8 – 8 – 8 – 8 +

Repeat around each time, weaving the chains over and under the first pass of this round as shown. Check that all of the weaving is perfect, and then tie the thread ends at the beginning of this pass.

If you tatted the center ring option with the long picots you may cut these picots at the center of the picot, and then even fray them if you wish.

THC, and then enjoy your beautiful flower. Make several that are identical and then add jewelry findings to make earrings, a necklace, or a broach.

This Poppy flower can be flat, as shown in the previous photos, or 3-D by pushing the center of the flower down while holding the outside rounds in place.

Poppy Leaf

Chain – 6 turn

Ring (3 – 3) turn

Chain 8 – 4 turn

Ring (3 – 3 – 3 – 3) turn

Chain 8 – 4 turn

Ring (3 – 3 – 3)

Ring (3 + 4 – 2 – 2 – 4 – 3)

Ring (3 + 3 – 3) turn

Chain 8 – 4 turn

Ring (3 – 3 – 3 – 3) turn

Chain 8 – 4 turn

Ring (3 – 3) turn

Chain 8 – 3 – 8 turn

This is the point of the leaf.

Continue the other side of the leaf in reverse order so it is a mirror image.

Ring (3 – 3) turn

Chain 4 – 8 turn

Ring (3 – 3 – 3 – 3) turn

Chain 4 – 8 turn

Ring (3 – 3 – 3)

Ring (3 + 4 – 2 – 2 – 4 – 3)

Ring (3 + 3 – 3) turn

Chain 4 – 8 Turn

Ring (3 – 3 – 3 – 3) turn

Chain 4 – 8 turn

Ring (3 – 3) turn

Chain 6 Weave the Celtic Twist then join to the first picot.

Poppy leaves are not symmetrical, and may be very different from each other much like dandelion leaves.

They can be long and thin in some places, but they all have this jagged appearance as shown here. They are tatted similar to the long leaf on page 8 With the Celtic Weave for the first round.

Next tat around the outside of the leaf joining where you wish to join and skipping picots when you wish. This is just a suggested outline. Make the leaves all different to be like real poppy leaves.
See the photo on the previous page.

Chain 10 + 6 + 5 + 2 + 6 – 4 + 5 + 6 – 6 + 5 + 2 + 2 + 4 + 6 – 4 + 8 – 8
The "8 – 8" is the point of the leaf outline.

Continue around the other side of the leaf in reverse order but feel free to change some of the stitch counts for variety as long as the leaf will still lie flat.

Chain + 4 – 6 + 4 + 2 + 2 + 5 + 6 – 6 + 5 + 4 – 6w + 2 + 5 + 6 + 10 +

To make the 3-D poppy flower you will also need one larger size bead in a light or very dark color. One smaller bead that is big enough to not go through the center of the larger bead. One floral wire stem for each flower. Floral tape to wrap the stem after the flower is assembled. Green thread.

You will need two or more dark color tatted center rings on page 11 for the center of the flower.

Assemble the 3-D poppy flower similar to the Poinsettia. Put a small bead on a piece of Thread and then put both thread ends through the larger bead.

Insert the threads through the center rings, through the petals, and then add a floral wire stem wrapped in floral tape around the wire and the base of the flower petals.

Continue wrapping the stem and add a few Poppy leaves on alternating sides of the wire randomly.

Celtic Rosebud

Instructions:

To begin: Wind about a yard of desired-color tatting thread on a tatting shuttle. Or use finger tatting for all three rings. I recommend that you use size 10 thread for the first try!

Center ring

Leave about 24" tail at the beginning of the first ring. This is used to tat the third ring.

Ring (14 – 1 – 1 – 14)

Close ring (three small- to medium-sized picots)
Leave about 1/8" space, do not turn.

Second ring

Ring (14 – 14)

Close Ring

Leave about 1/8" space, do not turn.

Third ring

Lay the right side ring on top of the center ring by folding it over as you would close a book. See below.

Turn the piece upside down and bring the thread end left at the beginning of the first ring (new shuttle thread) around the hand to form the loop for tatting this ring. The previous rings are held between the thumb and first finger of your left hand. (See illustration on the following page.)

Weave the shuttle thread through the first two rings as shown.

Ring (14 – 14) pull the DS through the first two rings.

The drawing below on the left shows the third ring in progress. It is held in the pinch between the thumb and first finger, but the thumb is not shown here so you can see the piece clearly. The thread end left at the beginning of the first ring is the NEW shuttle thread which goes around the hand then weaves through the first two rings as shown before beginning tatting the third ring.

The thread goes around the left hand just the same as making a normal ring. While tatting you should be able to tat as if it were just any old ring without worrying about the two other rings and the weaving.

Before closing this ring, pull the tatting through where the weaving goes.

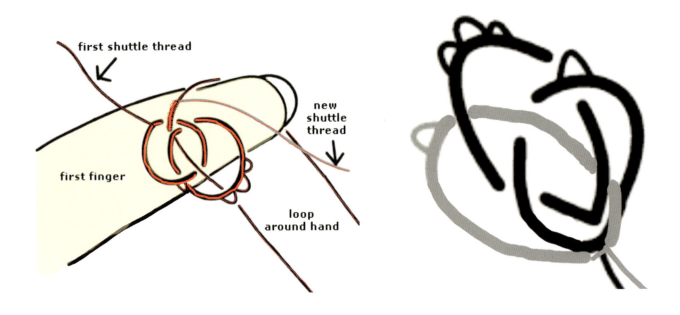

When the stitches and new shuttle thread are pulled through completely, close the ring and turn it right-side up again and arrange the rings so that the rosebud looks like the drawing on the right.

Finger tatting works well for this piece.

Sepals, Stem, and Leaves

Wind about a yard of green thread on a tatting shuttle. The base of the rosebud rings will be covered by the sepals (green leaves) which form a 3-D ring around the bottom of the rosebud.

Ring 1 (2 - 3 - 3) Close ring

Ring 2 (3 + 3 - 2) Close ring   Join to last picot of previous ring

Ring 3 (2 + 3 - 3) Close ring   Join to last picot of previous ring

Ring 4 (3 + 3 + 2) Close ring   Join to last picot of previous ring and the first picot of the first ring as shown below.

This photo shows the second join of the fourth ring to the picot of the first ring.

Notice how the piece is folded over to make it easy to do this join.

Finish tatting the rest of this ring after this join, and then close the ring.

Tie the two green thread ends in a square knot to finish the sepals.

Pull the thread ends from the rosebud through the middle of the sepals. Tie the two green thread ends and the two rosebud thread ends in an overhand knot and pull it tight enough so that the two pieces are held tightly in place.

Using the two rosebud thread ends as the shuttle thread and the two green ends as the ball thread,

Chain 2

Tat with one green thread and both rosebud thread ends.

Chain 5 turn

Using the one green thread tat a leaf.

Ring (3 – 5) turn

Chain 1

Put that green thread in with the rosebud thread ends and use the other green thread as the ball thread.

Chain 5 turn

Tat another leaf

Ring (3 – 5) turn

Chain 5

Put this green thread also in with the other three thread ends, and then tie them all in a double overhand knot. Make twisted cord with the thread ends to about the right length for a bookmark,

Tie them in another double overhand knot. Finally, trim the remaining thread ends about 2" long for a tassel, or use the thread ends to tie on a larger tassel.

Celtic Rosebud Heart

Tat one red rosebud and the sepals. Pull the red thread ends through the sepals as in the bookmark. Tie the two green thread ends and the two red thread ends in a knot pulling the red ends tighter so that what shows is just the green.

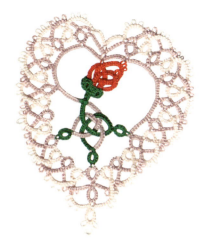

Celtic Knot Stem

Use the two red thread ends and one green thread end as the shuttle threads and the other green thread end on a shuttle as the ball thread.

Chain 2 – 25 turn

Ring (5 – 5) turn

Chain 25 turn

Ring (5 – 5) turn

Add the pink color on a shuttle and ball CTM as part of the shuttle and ball threads. Leave the red thread ends out one at a time, and then cut them off close to the work later.

Chain 25 turn

Ring (5 – 5) turn

Chain 25

Weave the Celtic Knot as shown with the green rings at the points of the knot. This knot is the same as the one on page 12. Join to the first picot of the stem. Tie the threads in an overhand knot, SLT. The shuttle and ball thread are pink. Leave the green thread ends out one at a time, after a few stitches and cut them off close to the work later.

Chain 10 – 8 – 8 – 8 – 8 + – 8 + – 8 – 8 – 8 – 8 – 8 +

The previous join is to the first green ring. Where the instructions have + – it means to join and make a picot at the same place.

Outline Round

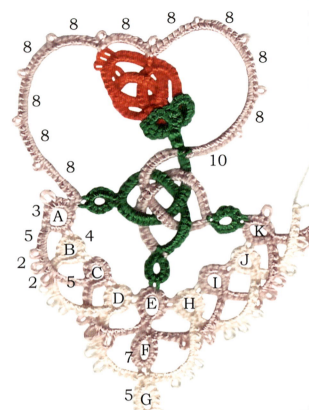

Ring A is a split ring so both threads need to be on a shuttle. Pull a couple of yards of pink from the ball and put it on a shuttle.

Split Ring A (3 – 3 / 3 – 3) turn

Chain 5 – 2 – 2 – 5 turn

Wind a yard or two of the cream color thread on a shuttle CTM.

Ring B (4 + 4 – 4) turn

Chain 5 – 2 – 2 – 5 turn

Notice how the cream and pink chains weave over and under each other. This is a Celtic interweave pattern.

Pink
Ring C (3 + 3 – 3 – 3) turn

Chain 5 – 2 – 2 – 5 turn

Cream
Ring D (4 + 4 – 4) turn

Chain 5 – 2 – 2 – 5 turn

Pink
Ring E (3 + 3 + 3 – 3)

Use the second pink shuttle "ball thread" for Ring F.

Ring F (7 – 7) turn

S1 Pink Chain 5 – 2 – 2 – 5 turn

40

**Cream Thread
Join to the picot of ring F turn   SLT**

Ring G (5 – 1 – 1 – 5)

SLT   Join to the picot of ring F   turn

Ring H (4 + 4 – 4) turn

Chain 5 – 2 – 2 – 5 turn

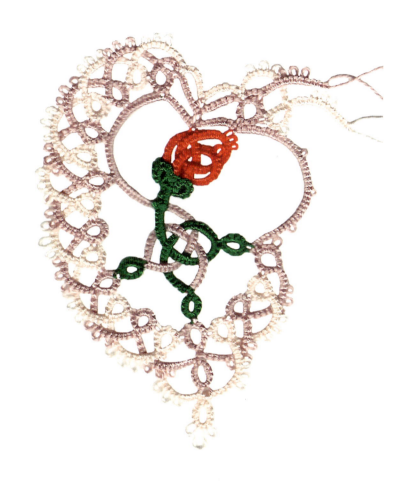

Alternate the pink and cream rings and chains as shown. Join each ring to the previous ring and the pink rings to the picots of the previous round as shown.

When you tat the pink ring at the top center left you will begin the chains for the top center of the heart.

Chain 4 + – 7 + – 7   turn

Ring (3 + 3 – 3 – 3)   turn

Chain 4 + 5 – 2 – 2 – 5

This previous ring is tatted differently from the other pink rings in that it is sideways. The top is the third picot. The join is to the previous round.

Next the cream thread goes across the top of the heart. **Join to the picot at the first + -   and then continue tatting the chain.**

Chain 7 + 7 + 5 – 2 – 2 – 5   turn

Ring (4 + 4 – 4)   turn

Chain 5 – 2 – 2 – 5

This is as far as is shown in the photo above.

41

Continue tatting the remainder of the rings and chains until you get to the beginning of the outside round. The last cream ring joins to the previous pink ring and the pink split ring that started the outline round.

THC   This heart may need to be blocked so that it keeps its shape.

Tatting completed, ends tied and ready to hide.

42

Stargazer Lily

I bought a bouquet of Stargazer lilies to use as a model to design this pattern, and watched them open.

The Stargazer Lily opens out completely flat with the ends of the petals curled under. It looks like a telescope gazing at the stars!

White Easter Lilies are More upright. Day Lilies and Asiatic Lilies are bright colors with lots of variation in colors.

The petals may or may not have bright spots on them. The ones that I bought had wonderful bright pink spots surrounded by a slightly lighter color of pink fading to pale, then white around the edge of the petals which ruffled slightly and turned under at the tips.

The center line of each petal has a strong vertical look, which I found very challenging to reproduce in tatting. The finished design is a Celtic Twist pattern that crosses over and under itself along the center of the petal, with darker spots, surrounded with a pale round, then white or ivory.

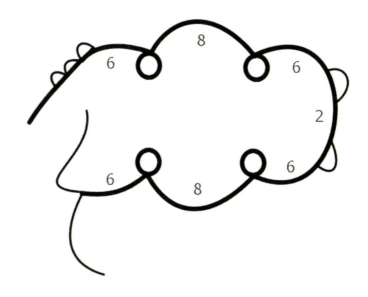

Start with about two yards of the darkest or brightest color thread on the shuttle. And the medium color thread as the ball thread.

43

Petals:
Round One

Chain (– 6 – 2 – 2 – 6) turn

Ring (3 – 3) turn

Chain (8) turn

Ring (3 – 3) turn

Chain (6 – 2 – 6) turn

Ring (3 – 3) turn

Chain 8 turn

Ring (3 – 3) turn

Chain (6)   STOP

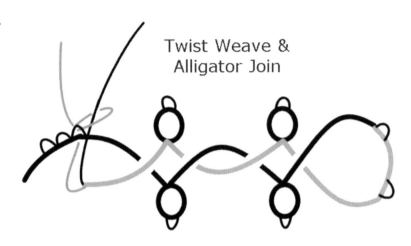

Twist Weave & Alligator Join

Do the Celtic Twist weave shown above, and then join to the last of the three picots of the first chain. Cut the chain thread leaving about 12" or so at the end.

Round Two Use the pale color for this chain.

Chain 8 + join to the first ring.

Chain 1 – 2 – 2 – 2 – 2 – 1 + Join to the second ring.

Chain 1 – 1 – 1 – 1 + Join to the first picot of the chain in round one.

Chain 1 – 1 – 1 – 2 – 2 – 1 – 1 – 1 + Join to the second picot of the chain in round one. Pull this chain tight before the second join so it forms a sharp point in the middle.

Chain 1 – 1 – 1 – 1 + Join to the third ring.

Chain 1 – 2 – 2 – 2 – 2 – 1 + Join to the fourth ring.

Chain 8 + join to the second picot of the first round.

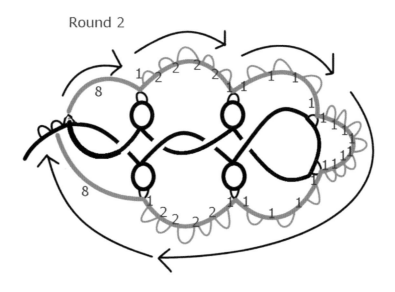

Cut the ball thread leaving about 12" at the end.

Round Three

**Use the white or ivory thread for this row.
Chain 10 + join to the first picot of row 2.**

Chain 1 – 1 – 1 – 1 + skip one picot of row 2, and join to the next.

Repeat the previous chain, skipping every other picot, and joining to the next all the way to the point of the petal.

Chain 6 – 2 – 2 – 6 + Join to the next picot at the point of the petal.

Repeat the row, which is a mirror image of the first half of this row.

Chain 1 – 1 – 1 – 1 + Repeat the previous chain, skipping every other picot

Chain 10 + Join to the first picot of the first row.

Chain 6 The is the first chain of the next petal.

Tat two more petals. This gives a group of three petals with six DS between them. Join to the first picot of the first petal to begin the third petal.

Round 3

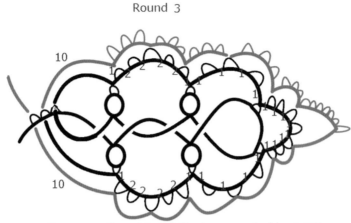

Same as other side. 3 Picots separated by 1 DS

When the third petal is completed tie the thread ends at the beginning of the third petal and trim them to about 12" long.

Tat another set of three petals, but begin with four DS instead of six, and tat only four DS between the petals..

Lily Center

Ring (1 – 1 – 1 – 2 – 2 – 1 – 1 – 2 – 1 – 1 – 2 – 2 – 1 – 1 – 1)

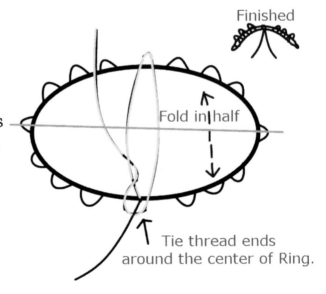

Close the ring, and fold it in half with the ends of thread at the center. Tie the ends around the ring to hold it flat. This is roughly the shape of a crescent moon.

Tat three of these rings for the pollen heads.

Assembling the Lily center

Pull about a yard of the thread from a ball of green (or whatever color of thread you wish to use for the filaments that hold the pollen heads upright) up through the middle of one of the folded rings and then back down on the other side.

Wind this thread onto a shuttle CTM.

Chain 35 – 6
Push the stitches tightly together so that This chain will be fairly stiff.

Chain 1 RDS – 1 RDS

Push these stitches tightly together.

Chain 6 – 35

Push these stitches tightly together.

Pull one thread end up through the second folded ring, and then back down through the other side. Tie the two thread ends to secure the folded ring. Pull one thread end back up through the folded ring.

Hide this end

Cut these ends the same length as the picots.

Hide the other thread end in the tatted chain, and trim the thread ends at the top of the folded ring about the same length as the picots of the folded ring.

47

Begin another pollen head as before.

Chain 35 - 6

Push the stitches tightly together so that
This chain will be fairly stiff.

Chain 1 RDS – 1 RDS

Push these stitches tightly together.

Chain 6 + 35 BDS

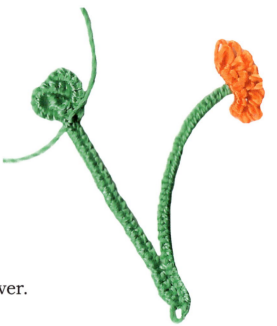

Push these stitches tightly together.

Pistil: This is in the very center of the flower.

Tie the thread ends in a square knot.

Chain – 25

Weave this chain into a Celtic Knot by tying it in an overhand knot but keep the Chains flat not twisted. See the photo above.

Tie the thread ends at the picot at the beginning of the Celtic knot, and then hide both of these thread ends in the tatted chains then cut them off close to the work.

Fold the two pollen-head piece in half so that both folded rings face the same direction. Place it beside the other piece with its' folded ring facing the opposite direction.

Thread a needle with the same thread as the chains and sew through the picots at the bottom, up between the chains, through all three picots, and then back down through the picots at the bottom to hold the flower center pieces all in place securely. Tie the thread ends in a square knot to secure them in place. Trim to about 12" long.

Assembling the Lily flowers

There are now three parts to the lily flower completed. The upper set of three petals with four DS between the petals, the center assembly, and the lower set of three petals with six DS between the petals.

Begin with the upper set of petals. Put one of the thread ends on a tapestry or yarn needle to weave in and out through the petals to hold them in place. Sew from the bottom through between the outer two chains of one petal.

Weave down and up and down and up between the chains near the bottom of the petal. Weave through all three petals finishing back where you began after the third petal.

Pull the woven thread as tight as you wish to hold the petals in place. The stargazer lily has its' petals out fairly flat, while the Day Lilies have them gathered more upright.

This weaving is shown in the photo here done with a thicker, contrasting color thread for clarity.

After weaving the thread through the chains, tie the thread ends together.

Insert the thread ends down through the center of this set of petals, and then through the center of the other set of petals. Tie the ends together.

Use one of the thread ends from the lower set of three petals and weave through one of these petals. Next, go under the chain in the center of an upper petal. Continue weaving through the next lower petal, and then under the center chain in the next upper petal.

Weave the thread through all six petals in this way. Pull the thread snug with the petals arranged equally around the flower. Now tie this thread end to the other thread end from the lower set of petals. Insert the thread ends through the middle of the flower.

Pull the thread ends from the center arrangement down through the center of the flower and, making sure that everything looks pleasing, tie the thread ends together at the base of the flower.

Add a floral wire stem and wrap the thread ends around the stem, then wrap it all with some floral tape.

Arrange several flowers in a vase for a lovely bouquet.

Day Lily

Day Lilies have petals that are usually orange or yellow. Some Day Lilies have a yellow stripe in the center of orange petals.

Tatting a solid color Day Lily is easy. Begin with one shuttle and ball CTM wound with orange or yellow thread.

To tat a Day Lily with a yellow stripe begin with orange thread on shuttle and ball CTM, but use yellow thread for the ball thread for the first round.

All of the rings are the same: Ring (3 – 3)

Chain – 6 – 2 – 2 – 6 turn Ring turn

Chain 8 turn Ring turn

Chain 8 turn Ring turn

Chain 8 turn Ring turn

Chain 6 – 2 – 6 turn Ring turn

Chain 8 turn Ring turn

Chain 8 turn Ring turn

Chain 8 turn Ring turn

Chain 6

Weave the Celtic Twist.

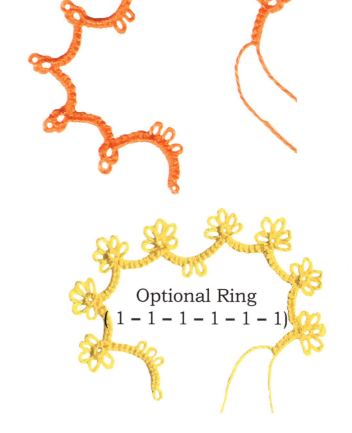

Optional Ring
(1 – 1 – 1 – 1 – 1 – 1)

Round Two

Alligator join to the third picot of round one.

Chain 8 + 1 – 2 – 2 – 2 – 2 – 1 + 1 – 2 – 2 – 2 – 2 – 1 + 1 – 2 – 2 – 2 – 2 – 1 + This join is just before the point of the petal.

Chain 1 – 1 – 1 – 1 + 1 – 1 – 1 – 1 – 1 – 1 – 1 – 1 +

Chain 1 – 1 – 1 – 1 + 1 – 2 – 2 – 2 – 2 – 1 + 1 – 2 – 2 – 2 – 2 – 1 +

Chain 1 – 2 – 2 – 2 – 2 – 1 + 8

Alligator join to the second picot of round one.

Round Three

Chain 10 + 1 – 1 – 1 – 1 +

Chain 1 – 1 – 1 – 1 +

Continue tatting three picots with one DS between them and joining to every other picot of round two until you get to the join to the third picot of the point of the petal.

Chain 6 – 6 +

Continue tatting three picots with one DS between them and joining to every other picot of round two until you get to the join to the final ring.

Chain 10 Alligator join to the first picot of round one.

Chain 6 This is the first chain of round one of the next petal.

Tie the ends to the beginning after the third petal of the set of three petals. Tat two sets of three petals. Also tat the center of the lily as in the Stargazer Lily and then assemble the Day Lily as described in the Stargazer Lily.

52

Star Flower

This flower has five petals tatted like the Lily petals, but with just the first two rows. The star flower is named Borage, or Bee Bread and comes in purple, pink and white.

Chain – 3 – 2 – 6
Continue with the first round of the petal.

Weave the Celtic Twist then alligator join to the third picot of the first chain. Tat the second round as in the Lily petal. Alligator join to the second picot of the first chain.

Chain 3 – 2 – 6   Continue tatting this petal.

After the fourth petal join to the first picot and then tat the last petal. Tie the ends at the beginning picot. Use one thread end to weave through the petals to hold them in place as shown on page 49.

Sepals

Green thread CTM on shuttle and ball.

Chain – 3 turn

Ring (5 – 3 – 3 – 5) turn

Chain 3 Turn

Ring (5 + 3 – 3 – 5) turn

Repeat rings and chains until there are four rings with chains between them. Join to the first picot.

The fifth ring is Split Ring (5 + 3 – 3 / 5)

Tie the ends in the first picot of the first ring. This makes it cup.

Chain 13 – 13 +   Repeat around. THC

Assemble with a bead tied on green thread for the center of the flower. Put these thread ends through the center of the five petals and then through the center of the sepals. Add a floral wire stem and wrap with floral tape.

Celtic Knot Dragonfly

You will need two 4 to 6 mm beads for the eyes. If using smaller or larger thread, use beads the best size for the thread.

Use any size tatting thread in two colors: one color for the wings, and the other color for the head, body, and tail.

This is a good project for finger tatting.

Head: Trefoil Celtic Knot

Chain – 10 bead 10 bead 10

Tie this chain in an overhand knot, but do not twist the chain. It must lie flat as shown in the photo above. Next tie the thread ends in a square knot through the picot to hold it in place. Trim the thread ends to about a yard long. Set this aside for now.

Wings: Make 4

Trefoil Celtic Knots Begin with a picot by tieing an overhand knot in the thread and tat the first stitch a picot's distance from the knot.

Chain - 3 then make 20 Picots with 3 DS between them, 3

Tie an overhand knot in the chain to make a trefoil knot like the head. Join the end to the beginning of this chain through the starting picot.

Chain 8 – 10 + 3 + 5 + 3 + 8 – 8 + 3 + 5 + 3 + 10

Join to the picots of the trefoil knot around the outside. Finally, tie the ends to the first picot of this outline leaving long tails about a yard long for the ends.

Dragonfly Body

Place two wings on a table with one thread end from each one going to the right and one thread end from each wing going to the left. Leave a space about six or eight inches from these two wings and place the other two wings alongside the thread ends from the first two wings with the thread ends going to the right and left like the first two.

You will need to be able to identify which thread ends come from the wings on the opposite side. Tie a knot at the ends of the thread ends, or use a hair clip to hold them together.

Place the Dragonfly head on the wing thread ends half way between the two sets of wings. Using the thread ends from the head, tat over the wing thread ends:

Chain 25 RDS Wing 1 RDS Wing

Repeat on the other side and then pull both sides of the wing thread ends from the opposite side carefully so that the wings slide right next to the wrapped stitches and the head is in the middle between them. It is helpful to have someone hold the wings while you do this.

Chain 25 RDS Repeat on the other side.

Weave the chains into a Celtic Knot, and then tie two of the wing thread ends in a square knot to hold the Celtic knot together.

Using the two thread ends from the head tat around the Celtic Knot.

Chain 8 + 8 + 8 + 8

These joins are all alligator joins where one thread goes over the wings, head, and wings, and the other thread goes under them, Pull the core thread to tighten up the stitches.

This will make the Celtic Knot curl up and look three dimentional. Tat 10 or 12 DS in the chain to make it lie flat if you wish.

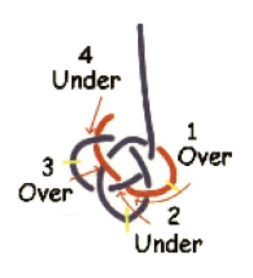

the previous chain and do not pull it up tight. The number of stitches depends upon the size of the thread. Ten DS or even 12 will do. The point is to go around the Celtic Knot of the body and hold everything in place while allowing it to lie flat.

Tail (Option One)

Split Ring (5 / 5)

Two of the wing threads are the carrying threads and the head threads are the knotting threads. The other two wing threads go through the middle of the split rings.

Repeat the split rings 3 more times or to the desired length for the dragonfly tail.

Ring (5 – 2 – 5)

THC (Tie, Hide the ends, Cut them close to the work)

Tail (Option Two: Pearl tatting)

Gather all the threads, except for one of the thread ends from the head, for the carrying threads and use the thread from the head to tat RDS over the carrying threads. This is like the second half of a split ring.

5 RDS with head thread

Put this head thread into the carrying threads and use one of the wing threads to tat over the carrying threads.

5 RDS with wing thread

Push these stitches tightly together, then repeat with each color. Decrease the number of stitches to make smaller stripes towards the end of the tail.

Tie all the threads in a double overhand knot at the end of the tail, and then cut them to about 1/4" for a short tassel.

Balanced Double Stitch – BDS

HOW TO TAT LARGE RINGS AND LONG CHAINS THAT LOOK GOOD

Tatting, by the mathematical nature of the double stitch, curves around in loops and circles. It does this even if we don't want it to! The field of mathematics called topology actually defines knots in math equations.

OH NO!!! Not math!

I know a number of tatters reading this have just turned green, and then pale. You don't have to be able to do the math to benefit from what it offers. Just like you don't have to understand how a television set works to enjoy watching your favorite shows. Whew!

We can tat loosely and end up with floppy rings and chains that require blocking and stiffening to hold their shape. Or we can have tatting that twists and ruffles and doesn't have a lot of eye appeal. We can design with only smaller rings, and chains that curve, or short chains that will lie nearly straight.

BUT... if we want to tat something with very large rings, or long chains, that is a terrible tatting trouble.

Here is a Celtic Knot bat that I taught at the Fringe Element tat days two years ago. There are chains that are 60 stitches that bend in both directions. There are chains over 100 stitches long that curve around just so. I really struggled with the design of this piece, and my first 4 months of attempts were not pretty, and they will never be seen. They went directly into the circular file. Until – Eureka! My husband tied a sliding square knot for me. This is a knot used in rock climbing.

Here is the problem:

The tatting double stitch, pictured here, has the core thread with the knots made around it. Above the core thread there are 4 cords in the knot.

Below the core there are just 2. So when the stitches are pushed together there is an angle of about 12 degrees. This can be simply pictured as how the hour and minute hands on a clock look at 2 minutes before noon.

That's not a LOT of difference, unless we take that shape and put many of them side by side: like long tatted chains, and large rings.

Fig. A: Ring 35, Chain 35
This looks nice, but notice that the chain curves into about the same shape as the ring.

Fig. B: Ring 60, Chain 60 The ring wants to "ruffle" or twist, and the chain curves around nearly twice.
It can be tatted loosely to make it lie flat, but then it is floppy, and must be stiffened and blocked.

Fig. C: This is a ring of 60 stitches tatted with the Balanced Double Stitch Like the long chains in my bat, these stitches hold their shape without blocking or stiffening, and they do not ruffle, or twist.

Here is the solution:

This is a sliding square knot used in rock climbing and ship rigging. Done in tatting, it's a Balanced Double Stitch. There are 4 cords below the core thread, and 4 above, with the extra loops around the core sitting inside the waistband or bump of the stitch. Notice that there is much less of an angle to this knot. It can bend equally up or down.

When many of them are pressed together they can be shaped straight, or in a curve in either direction. No stiffening or blocking is necessary.

The ring of 60 BDS, shown in Fig. C on the previous page, is just 60 of this knot tatted tightly. The long chains in the bat are possible using this stitch, whereas with a normal DS, they flipped, and flopped, and twisted all over and ended flopping the bat into the trash can!

How do I tat a BDS? For each half of the balanced double stitch, go around the core thread a second time before tightening the half stitch.

Tatting the BDS in needle tatting is easy to do. Just wrap the thread around your finger two times instead of once and then put the tatting needle through the two wraps. Do this for each half of the stitch, and you will have the same effect as shuttle-tatted BDS.

There has been some discussion about a sentence from the book, Tatting, by Rhoda Auld published in 1974.

This book contains many inovative ideas which are worthy of note including; combining tatting with macrame and bobbin lace, Zig Zag chains, and adding beads to tatting.

She encouraged tatters to experiment with the tatting techniques and try new ideas. We tatters owe a debt of gratitude to this brilliant lady.

"I formed a ring of double stitches by doubling each half of the knot. This resulted in a solid, chunky ring that looked as though it might contrast well with the ordinary knot. Therefore, I worked a series alternating first one kind of ring and then the other, and joining them together (fig. 6-3e), but, although the new ring took up more space, there was not really enough difference to show."

Auld, Rhoda L. Tatting. New York. Van Nostrand Reinhold Co. 1974. Print. 84-85.

Made in the USA
Lexington, KY
10 July 2014